£ 1.99

17/49
Fa

ON THE NATURE OF MAN

DAGOBERT D. RUNES

ON THE NATURE OF MAN

An Essay in Primitive Philosophy

PHILOSOPHICAL LIBRARY
New York

CONTENTS

THE QUEST

As I write these lines, and as you read them, we find ourselves aware of living in an ocean of energies. We are much like a tree in the forest, visibly growing from sapling to huge ripe trunk. As time goes on, we wither away, dry and lifeless, unless some blight cuts us down before our time.

What is man, beyond the awareness of shooting up for a while from parental roots into a being like his parents, then growing to be like his grandparents? And there the drama ends, except that man too sets out seedlings for tomorrow's growth.

Still, we are not mere plants. We are animals prowling for food and shelter. We move about restlessly. Yet we are not mere animals either, forever on the hunt unless asleep—we are imbued with an awesome feeling of nature beyond the touch of paw and nose, of tongue and tooth, of ear and eye. The trees turn knowingly with the wind; spiders spin webs cunningly; but we fashion thoughts and tales and tartans in zigzags and spires which wander and rise far beyond their use and purpose.

We are spiritual.

We are plants inspired by unpredictable notions of useless games, by intricate laws and bizarre morals that give us more unease than comfort; by fanciful cogitations about invisibilities—we are full of mysteries that, at least to our perception, trouble neither tree nor tapir.

What goes on in the core of our mind, this tumult created of our vexation with the business of animal living, lies just in our mind. Our mind is our whole world; the whole world is in our mind.

Our sculpture is just a rock to the bird, our painting only a greasy canvas to the cat, our songs scarcely a noise to the fish, and the words spouting from our lips—what are they to the tree?

To a city of ants, a destructive rip of the bulldozer means the end of the world; perhaps to a shoal of fish, the draining of a pool means the Great Drought; to a stranded herd of sheep the river's overflow in spring is the Everlasting Flood; and to the worm in a stomach there is no world outside those walls.

Man splits some atoms and talks of harnessing the universe. Which universe? Which one of the infinite universes?

Man, little two-legged man, riding like a fungus on an elephant at breathless speed on this uncontrollable gigantic rock vehicle through endless space in aeonic time—man finds himself aware of some few of the unfathomed energies of this little globe, and in his mind he appears nature's master, *deus ex machina*.

The homing pigeon which finds its way high above a hundred miles of broken landscape, the bat which flies in the black of night, the salmon which crosses an ocean against fearful obstacles, the tiny caterpillar which spins an almost perfect cocoon, the day-old chick which pecks a grain instead of a pebble—they all, and many million others from microbe to gorilla, live under manifold energies as strange to us as the turning of the green plant to the sun.

Certainly there are quick and quack answers

to every query. It is amazing how rapidly shallow explanations come forth. Sometimes men even think they solve a problem by giving it a Greek or Latin name.

We are shipwrecked on this watery, germ- and microbe-infested splinter of a minor star and are just another growth on it, shifting for food and shelter. And after all is said and done, today as in the age of the stilt-dwellers, the days of man are still devoted to the lowly purpose of digging for food and toiling for shelter.

But man is spiritual.

Man must ponder. He ponders his past and learns from mistakes as well as successes; he ponders his future in looking back at his past; he ponders the lines on the horizon and the lines on the face of his mate; he ponders the thunder and lightning, the sun, the moon and the stars, the heaving ocean and the rising mountains, the green of the faraway valley and the blooming sweetness of the flowers, the fury of the howling beasts and the uncertainty about his neighbor—man ponders, and from his meditations, his fears, his loves and anguish, spring helpful faith and philosophies, lawful union and the manners of comfortable living.

This is all man's world in man's mind; man's mind *is* man's world.

To the timeless universe coursing through infinite space, what is this all but the dreams and doodlings of a blade of grass in the evening wind?

That which man calls "beauty"—what is it? That which man calls "knowledge"—what is it? What man calls "moral"—what is it? What he calls "heritage"—what is it? The blade of grass is singing in the wind and it thinks the wide, wide universe hearkens.

Man must still live as if his world were real and perennial, but if he finds his true and tiny measure, a better man he may be—more humble, more kind, more forgiving, more hesitant.

Hesitance is the beginning of philosophy, and charity its end.

THE HEM OF THE GODS

We can but touch the hem of the gods. I presume it behooves us to interpret our narrow milieu as well as we can, as well as we can see and comprehend it. And frequently, in trying to piece together this jigsaw puzzle, we throw in a hypothesis, or even a word, where a part of the facts is missing—a new synthetic word which makes some people feel they have the answer, though they have only a word.

A Greek philosopher in ancient days mused that if horses and cows and fish could think, they probably would picture their gods as horses, cows, and fish. Humans are no different. They imagine the world has come about by creation or spontaneous generation for the sake of humans, with humans as the universe's crowning diadem. Religious teleologies and evolutionary rationalism are, on this issue, brothers of one skin.

Man is as little the final purpose of divine providence as an elk or a beetle or a salamander. By the same token, the popular ladder of evolution from fish through amphibia, reptiles, and mammals to sterling man is equally anthropomorphic and monotheistic.

I cannot tell whether a skunk be a higher level creature than a trout, or whether a clam rank above a bee, or whether in the great order of things Hitler be placed above a nervous orangutan in the zoo.

I presume the antelope regards the gamekeeper, who feeds him in winter and waters him during the dry season, as some sort of demigod and spells out to his offspring the smell and step of the gun-toting hunter as the devil incarnate—such is his theology. Perhaps the barracuda in the ocean considers himself as being at the summit of evolutionary development since he can pretty much master the waters of the bay, except for the tricky barbed hooks from hell above; for to the barracuda there is heaven below and the devil overhead.

Man will naturally make his own hells and

heavens, as will other animals, and feel himself cock of the evolutionary roost.

All animals are mere creatures living in the ocean of oxygen and hydrogen, or in the ocean of plain oxygen. They procreate in a similar manner, usually by fertilizing eggs within the body or without; they eat the same kinds of grubs; they suffer from like ailments, and perish by disintegration and disease, unless they kill each other before their natural lifetime has expired. Whole organs of man and animals are so much alike they could almost be interchanged. Perhaps some day they will be; some animal glands have already been transplanted successfully into humans.

There are some reasons for man to feel that he may be the epitome of the universe; man has become aware of quite a few sources of energy; most of which he has used immediately to destroy other men. But it is not unreasonable to assume that some insects have learned to manage sources of energy unknown to man which they use, for instance, to carry loads many hundred times heavier than themselves. Their use of strength as well as ingenuity is often applied to gathering a supply of food for their settlements.

These and many parallel considerations fail to inspire me with the idea that there is such a process in nature as evolution toward perfection. And even if evolution is taking place, the goal of its progress is positively not man.

When writers, clear-thinking or otherwise, set up a whole plausible system of probabilities and likelihoods, there is a danger that some lazy-minded epoch will take cover under this comfort-able philosophy and stay there like a worm that has crawled into an empty snail shell. It is so pride-warming and satisfying to think: fish, am-phibian, reptile, mammal and, finally, glorious rational man!

But there are fish swimming the seas today whose ancestors lived millions of years ago. Some spunky paleontologist sets down the exact num-ber of years, which he has derived with remark-able accuracy; one almost expects to be given the hour and day of birth of the "151,000,000-year-old" fishbone.

These fish, after all the millions of years of

evolution, are still fish, and the rats, with all their cross-breeding, are still rodents, and the mosquitoes are still vermin. And the orangutan will never beget anything but another ape, no matter what.

There are some changes within breeds, but the true answer has not been found; only a plausible hypothesis has been advanced. Even if all the evolutionary alibis are accepted, there is still the one basic query: Wherefrom the gases, or rocks, or greens whence the majestic panorama around us developed—the waters, the hills, the billions of moving things?

Wherefrom the spark that kindled the fire of the sun of suns?

We stand here before a riddle. There are quick and ready answers to this one, too. But, to those who hesitate before they finish a thought, the riddle remains.

MAKER OF THE ALPHABET

We do not know when man began. The bone and skull structure of the most primitive bushman differs little from that of a contemporary scholar of the same continental group. There has been a lot of shallow guessing in connection with a few unearthed human bone fragments.

The fact is, we know next to nothing about man's origin.

Our findings of man's "early" existence are only about eight thousand years old and center around clay and stone tablets in the Middle East. Although our historians have classified everything before the last fifteen hundred years as "antiquity," in the face of the great uncharted era of man's past the whole eight thousand years can be safely lumped together in one big little bit, the "Alphabet Period" of man. The clay literature of the Sumerians, for instance, nearly five thousand years old, is as good as most of the

law-penning or social scripture of our day. Whoever wrote those pieces, whoever, even earlier,
prepared the art work found near Jericho, was
as good a craftsman with pencil or brush as we
have today.

The man of five or six or eight thousand years
ago—certainly the many men who left the imprint of their engraving—were people of our own
caliber and virtues, whatever these may be. The
amazing thought is the casual demeanor of these
men of antiquity who set down their literary
output and bits of their spiritual heritage. They
neither were nor felt themselves to be great
original thinkers or discoverers; they merely
looked upon themselves as diligent epigones.

There is no reason to assume that before the
Alphabet Period man was less of a human than
those who came after him. Writing as well as
sculpting is not a necessity of life in an isolated
or even tribal existence. Man living in a family
or small community in the forest, in the hills, or
on an island may go on for a million years without
ever thinking of the necessity of "engraving,"
which is the original meaning of writing. Abo-

rigines in Africa and Australia, as well as in the Arctic regions, had lived for immeasurable periods of time when first discovered by Europeans and had never known writing or reading, except for some pictures scraped on perishable wood. Yet the same people, when taken as slaves or trophies to other continents by cultured alphabetics of the Western world, quickly adapted themselves. They were not inferior fundamentally, nor were their anatomy and physiology primitive. They did not write because they had no need to write in their bush or igloo life. For all—or the very little—we know, African and Australian man may have lived in his wild habitat for a million years, leaving us nothing but a thought to ponder.

The Africans and Australians lived in tolerable social conditions until Messrs. Livingstone and Cook presumed upon them, and as for the Eskimos, they were a cheerful fishing and hunting lot whose language significantly had no word for "war." Among the aborigines there were some few—very, very few—who engaged in human sacrifice, but this practice was rather common among the ultra-literate nations of Greece and Rome. The Romans staged slaughter-fests to amuse not only the plebs, but even more, the aristocrats. It was customary for visiting Roman consuls and generals to be entertained by imaginative killings of captives and slaves.

There is nothing in the life of the illiterate aborigines to indicate their fundamental inferiority to the wantonly cruel civilized beings of the last five thousand years. Highly developed men carried on farming, fishing and hunting for endless years without leaving a trace but their bones, and these may have disappeared on the pyre or in the dust of the earth.

Limiting man's existence to a period beginning with engraving in caves or on clay means raising runes and ruins above their proper place as latter-day incidentals in the sheer endless stretch of man's inhabitance of this globe. Perhaps the ice sheets shifted thousands of years ago, and some day we may find under the icecaps the skeletons of men who looked like you and me —and still no alphabet and no vases and no painted skulls.

ETHICS AND ENERGY

It is barely two lifetimes since man encountered a group of new sources of energy, the knowledge of which made him appreciably change his ways of working and living. The harnessing of steam, of oil, of electricity, and finally of atomic energy revolutionized his production and distribution systems. At the same time, the accidental discovery of anesthetics and of the microbic nature of disease wrought changes in his healing methods.

Before this recent leap into some of the many ways and byways of nature, the man of the year 1800 A.D. lived in a world very much like that of the man of 1800 or 3800 B.C.

Throughout the Alphabet Period, until the early years of the eighteenth century, people plowed and traveled with the help of horses, mules and oxen, fought wars with edged weapons, sometimes using the earlier catapult and the later cannon, let the wind in their sails push them across the waters, put up walls and towers for protection, let kings and upstarts enslave them, wrote pretty poems, long epics, religious precepts and moral admonitions masterminded by royal priests and priestly kings—but no novels. The personalized narratives of the commoner had to wait for the eighteenth century.

The surgeon, prior to the middle of the nineteenth century, could do little but perform hasty amputations for his shocked and quaking patients, and the physician knew nothing of the true microbic nature of disease. A man with a serious infection was no safer with a physician of 18th century London than he was with a Sumerian healer of the year 2500 B.C.

As for some of the major social isms of the 18th century in the Western world and the year 1800 B.C. in Babylon, it may be said that many citizens of our continent would have found the ancient laws of Hammurabi much too encroaching on their privileged status with regard to slavery, debt-collection, misuse of bondsmen, etc.

:-:

The alphabet is the great spreader of factual information. Without the alphabet, intelligence is limited to one person or a small group. Considerable knowledge in the sciences and crafts must have been lost in earlier centuries through lack of the written word. And since knowing begets knowledge, the written word constantly widened the circle of the knowing. And from the growing masses of the knowing mushroomed the rising light of the last few centuries.

The man of the year 5000 B.C. differed but little in his ways from the man of almost 2000 A.D.—true. Only in our days there are a thousand million men who live in awareness, or partial awareness, of present-day knowledge, while in those early years only a very few were informed. Man's thinking has not changed, but more men—many, many more men—think. Yet in great areas of the globe their thinking is less free today than it was then.

Man today may let his thoughts wander freely over his mechanical problems, but in the sensitive spheres of social, political and moral action there are hard and tyrannical taskmasters abroad who prescribe his every idea and word. These demagogues think themselves Christ-Gods, and in Draconic fashion send out their officious propaganda (*pro paganis*— "to the pagans").

THE FURTIVE HUNTER

Of the animate organisms on this globe, there appear to be these few kinds: plants that live on minerals, and parasitic fungi that live on other plants; animals that live on plants, and animals that live on other animals as well as plants. Man belongs to this last category; in fact, man lives on all—minerals, vegetables, and animals.

We know by fossil evidence that most ancient plants, such as blue-green algae, fungi, and flagellata looked very much like present-day growths of the same kind. The preserved structures of prehistoric animals indicate that mammals were similar to those of our own period. The whole issue of selective evolution becomes rather hypothetical in view of the almost unchanged character of algae, molds, and fungi through all of a billion years.

What was man like a million years ago? We do

not know. We do not even know whether the so-called savages found by the discoverers of the 15th, 16th, and 17th centuries in Africa and Australia were truly wild men, since they may have been reached hundreds or thousands of years before by alphabetic Europeans or Asiatics who may have given them spear and bow and other implements as well as some practical information. They did not give them the alphabet, since the natives in their tribal existence had absolutely no use for it.

The earliest findings in camps and caves point to man as a user of flint weapons and tools, and as an eater of the meat of horse and reindeer. Beyond that, we know nothing. For analogy, we may perhaps draw on the aborigines of Australia and Africa at the time of their discovery by the Europeans.

Man of the "Tool Age," that is before the Alphabet Period, very likely lived in the manner of a native of darkest Australia in the 17th century. He used some primitive tools and weapons to sustain himself. He accumulated no intelligence, since he had no means or desire or even opportunity to assemble or preserve ideas aside from those he put to immediate use. If by sheer observation an individual came across a bit of information or a new type of workable tool, it was bound to die with him or his next of kin. There was no way, and no incentive, to spread knowledge beyond the borders of the immediate tribe. Had a bush African a hundred thousand years ago seen the principle of the wheel in nature—for example, two round stones with flattened sides rolling down an embankment—what earthly use could he have found for a wheel in his jungle existence?

Man a million years ago—what was he like? There is no reason to assume that naked man would live anywhere but in the warmer climates. He was naked; he had no tools, no weapons; he could not devour skin-covered animal flesh. Without tools, he was unable to snare and kill animals, fish, or fowls; he had to grind his food. Very likely ancient man lived on grain, fruits and roots. Perhaps he attached himself to other herbivorous animals, such as cattle, horses, reindeer. Perhaps he learned to steal their milk as he "grazed" alongside them. Those peaceable and gentle animals may have domesticated man before he turned around and domesticated his milk-givers. Maybe he learned to eat their flesh after they fell dead. Perhaps he first cut the cadaver into pieces with a flint, and ground the meat between rocks to make it edible. Possibly, after a brush fire struck his abode, he found, on returning, the carcass of an animal burned to death, tasted the burned, tenderized flesh, and liked it—and so learned a new diet which changed him into a carnivore.

Naked man was more like a goat than a tiger. With his bare hands, man was limited to grains and fruits. Not until he found tools and weapons was he able to go on the hunt for flesh.

We may never know what changed naked, bare-handed, grain-eating man into a tool- and weapon-handling hunter and farmer. Naked man is perhaps the most helpless creature in free nature. He is the only animal that cannot scent other animals, the presence of water, the whereabouts of food. Unlike any other animal, he could starve in the nearness of plenty.

What makes man so dumb and awkward? He is too slow to catch either deer or hare; he is too weak to fight either wolf or leopard; he could neither eat nor digest wool-covered lamb; on his own, he does not even know a berry from poison.

Without weapons, ancient man of the pre-tool period could have existed only on easily accessible grains and fruits. The only meat available to him was rotting carcasses and insects. It is interesting that even today some isolated tribes of central Africa live on just such a diet of fruits, grains, and ground-up cadavers and ants.

Such, and no better, was ancient man.

There is a wisdom of the body in all animals: the ant building its intricate tunnel cities, the spider weaving its clever webs, the mollusk crawling into a shell and dragging it about itself for protection, the opossum playing dead, and so on. Ancient man may have had some such instinctive wisdom. But how, from those instincts, the handling of tools and weapons developed, we may never know. We must assume that Mother Nature was the teacher, and that all of man's early tools and weapons are to be found in the wild.

A hanging vine caught in a branch becomes a catapult if a stone or stick lodges in it. A broken vine near an embankment becomes a rope for sliding or swinging. A rock used for grinding a tough cadaver may almost propel itself against an enemy from the hands of one surprised. Other animals have found sticks and stones lying about and used them for defense and attack. However, to store sticks and stones for later use is another and tremendous step in body-wisdom which, of all the animals, was taken only by man.

To dig for roots is common to many animals, but to set grain into holes which have been dug in the earth is no doubt the longest step in man's advance from a crawling grubber of edibles to master of the green.

Man may have seen the wind blow grain about and watched new grain sprout days later. He then may have playfully copied Mother Nature and dug holes so the wind could not blow the seed away.

Man learned from nature by mere observation and repetition. Man could have learned to throw a pointed stick as he learned to throw a rock.

And when his stone or flint became sharp and thin from grinding flesh, he may have learned to use the flint on the end of a pole or alone as a knife, and the flint on a pole became a spear or an arrow or an axe. That in grinding flesh man would create sparks and set nearby dry leaves afire was unavoidable.

And here we may have the all of man's tools, weapons and prerequisites, which he used for unaccountable thousands of years and, in truth, still uses in places as the equipment serving life's necessities.

Man seems to have lived merely with spear, axe and fire for all the ages and thrived on it, checking the animals, raising more grains and fruits, even fashioning nets in the style of spider webs to catch fish. Man did all that, and frequently with greater family and tribal unity than we can pride ourselves on today.

Some ten thousand or more years ago, however, man began to put words on clay and stone. With this began the Alphabet Period, and the gathering and spreading of intelligence. Man no longer waited for a glimpse of nature's secrets, often overlooked and quickly forgotten. He now set down for others what he saw or thought, and where there had been only one idea brightening a single man's mind for his brief span of life, there now came together a thousand ideas in a thousand different men by means of the engraved word. And human knowledge grew by leaps and bounds.

But with all the many, many secrets man could now take from Mother Nature and keep—did this new intelligence make him a better man? Or is man—no longer naked, no longer helpless, no longer dumb—still on the prowl for conquest?

THE RIDDLE OF THE MOUTH

Man's most mysterious organ is the mouth. He uses his legs to walk as other animals; his arms to grasp, strike or embrace as other creatures use their front paws; but his mouth is more than a toothed opening to his stomach, designed to force down food.

Man's weak-jawed, horse-toothed mouth is the great riddle of the plains. Man can speak.

Some animals can grunt, or growl, or screech, or squawk, or bark or purr, or whistle, or howl. They can give off sounds of pleasure, fear or threat growing from their feasts or lusts. But man can speak.

What is speech?

Again we may assume that Mother Nature was man's teacher. Weak as naked man was, in his cave he may have blown like the wind to indicate to his mate the gusts outside; he may have hissed to signify a snake and roared to warn of a lion; he may have imitated the sound of running water, thunder, and crackling fire to communicate his awareness or wishes.

How many hundred thousands of years this process went on before it developed in man a vocabulary of the necessary few hundred words of language, we can only guess—most of the "figures and facts" concerning early man are not much more than guesses.

It is reasonable to assume that a long time before naked man could speak, all of man's tribes lived together. Later, perhaps because of gigantic earth upheavals, the tribes spread apart.

Man's speech is not an unavoidable sequitur of his existence. Man might have lived forever without this miracle, and miracles do not repeat themselves over and over again. None of the aborigines of the far continents were ever found to be without speech. And despite all philological attempts to break down languages into groups, the fact remains that speech itself is the most common denominator of all peoples. The tongue that could speak and not just swallow is the great wonder of man's far-off antiquity. Such a wonder could have happened only once.

Where? how? when? The answer fails.

The Alphabet Period increased the vocabulary of man from perhaps three hundred words to half a million. Enlargement of the language was part of the accumulated culture of that period. What matters is that the three hundred basic words found among all peoples from Borneo to Alaska and from Chile to Sakhalin are pretty much the same. The sound and fury of the bellowing cavemen or tree-dwellers may have been different, but their later speech levels us to an early togetherness on one common continental sector.

We do not know when man began to form sounds into speech and when he began to use tools. Time-guesses, based on geological parallels with unearthed bits of bone, such as Piltdown(?), Java, Peking, Neanderthal, etc., are utterly unreliable. In most cases we cannot be certain there is no fraud or slovenly speculation. Skull-sections and other bone fragments of apes have been hastily classified as human remains by scholars who were more emphatic than cautious.

In reality, man's time clock before the Alphabet Period is a book with seven seals to us, showing its face only to philosophical imagination, whether the face be true or false.

We do know that some time in the distant past naked man was born or shocked into an existence that was different from that of all other creatures on the globe. And no matter how much the visualized figure of early man differs from that of a present-day Western world citizen, he must have been close to unalphabetic, naked bush-Australian or African of the post-medieval era. To judge from the astonishing adaptability of the bush natives, their ability to absorb information without difficulty and almost instantly acquire all the technical and theoretical arsenal of modern man, we may conclude that ancient man had the brain and the latent body skills of modern man, ready to tackle most, if not all, of the tasks of our epoch.

How man came to such intrinsic wisdom, we do not know. Nor do we know whether such human wisdom rates high or low on the scale of the countless universes of which we see only one.

We are, after all, like the coral growing at the bottom of a small bay which sees a tiny bit of floating marine life, and feels, perhaps, "Such is Life, such is the World!"

But we know better. We know of a thousand bays in a thousand lakes and seas, and a thousand areas beyond the waters, beneath them and above.

What we see is only a tiny segment of life, moving as well as fixed, animated as well as petrified, on the bottom of an ocean of space. The far glimpses we get from this awkward position are like a fish-eye view of the water's surface. This is not *the* world we see, but just *our* world, our little bay in one of the universes.

A million years ago on a starry night man may have stood at the top of a hillock and peered into the glittering sky. What is beyond those faraway constellations, those recurring conglomerations? Ancient man gave them names after familiar animals: the Bear, the Ram, the Lion.

We peer at the same stars, plus some which ancient man could not see with the naked eye. Still we cannot answer his question any better

31

than he could. What is beyond those faraway constellations? And what is beyond those beyond? Is there an end? And how can there be?

The thought of a universe limited or unlimited is equally unacceptable to man's mind—like that other perennial riddle: how can all Beings evolve from Nothing? Even if we were to accept the childish concept of man as the crown of existence, how did man evolve from next-to-nothing? And if he did, whence came next-to-nothing?

These two riddles will ever be in need of solution.

And if we have to accept the concept of Divine creation, I would rather have it that the gods created man, thinking man, than that man evolved from some protoplasm or microbe or malodorous gas. And since we do not know what stirs in the faraway heavens, billions of miles and billions of years beyond our little animalistically limited capacities, I would rather fancy some mysterious Creator than more quadrillions of radiating particles and uncomprehending gases.

Gases explain nothing—for who is to explain the gases?

Man will never fathom the self-creation of gases, just as he will never be able to conceive of infinite gases of self-created origin. He might as well ponder on a bed of thought that is more restful and arresting.

Perhaps there is a wise little coral at the bottom of the bay which philosophizes: I don't pretend to know more than the other corals, but this I feel—there are many worlds beyond the surface of the bay; I can't even guess what they are like with my little coral brain, but I just know they are there.

Perhaps there is such a coral.

PUZZLING GODS

Man's thinking is so organized that he must find or imagine causality for all that he perceives. The dog or fish or bird may return with clocklike regularity to a feeding that repeats itself, but man must find the moving cause of what he discerns.

Naturally, as his knowledge grows his imagination diminishes, and vice versa. Sometimes, however, he seems to hanker for a super-cause of events in addition to the individual visible ones. He may, for instance, have a good understanding of the electrical phenomena causing lightning, or of the mechanics of rain—and still believe in direct intervention by an anthropomorphically imagined supernatural Being who would consider sparing man's personal home from the electric spark and his personal crop from the cloudburst.

Early man, endowed with pretty much the same mechanics of the mind as contemporary man, had to resort to the play of imagination when his wits gave out. For all that he perceived and failed to comprehend, he postulated an unknown "causer." Man's limited and still searching mind compulsively grasps for a postulate or hypothesis when no other explanation is available. In this sense, early man's reasoning was sound logic.

Illogic begins, as in modern man, when the chemical, electrical and other "causers" present themselves. And superstitious contemporary man continues to superimpose fantastic spirits over natural events by some peculiar sense of piety that makes him forever pray and beg personal favors of an entirely fictitious celestial manager of the very mundane affairs of the day.

Ancient man saw the wind shake loose a fruit or felt the fire singe his toe. All that, he comprehended, but he could not understand what made lightning, what drove the storms over the ocean waves, what made a tiny seed grow into a big tree, what made the stars sparkle in the dark, or the sun glow during the day.

So he found causes in his own puzzled soul:

gods. Since he could not picture a being outside his own world, the world of men and beasts, he endowed his gods with the qualities of both. The gods of ancient man were people, but better, stronger, quicker. They could fly like birds, swim like fish, travel like the swiftest of the animals. The gods of the Greeks, the Babylonians, and the Carthaginians, as well as the angels of later peoples, were but traditional carry-overs from the mythological fantasies of ancient man, with his flying tigers, human-headed horses and lions. Even the prehistoric animals lived on in the tales of dragons and giant birds.

Ancient man knew, as even some animals do, that you can sometimes pacify a threatening enemy by leaving him some of your food. Fearing these threatening powers of fire, water and air, ancient man would leave some food for the god-enemy, preferably where he suspected him of dwelling—under a large tree which had been struck by lightning, on a huge rock that had rolled dangerously down the hill, or at the shore where the waves had ripped apart his nets.

Thus did man make his first sacrifice to God-enemy, in an effort to pacify him as he would other enemies, man or beast. And when man became talkative he would say some words of homage and subservience to God-enemy, which he had learned to say to stronger men to whom he paid tribute.

Prayers and tributary worship began in man's fear of God-enemy; they were born of animal-instinctive offerings to an unknown and seemingly powerful creature.

The almost unbelievable tragi-comedy lies in the fact that today in an age of lightning deflectors, river dams, scientific navigation devices, and chemotherapy, men still make offerings to God-enemy to keep away lightning from their bodies, floods from their homes, storms from their ships, and microbes from their children. As if God-enemy were really roaming through the ether-envelope of this globe, ready to smite men for no good reason at all, and all that could stop his mischievous doings were a heartfelt prayer with a hymnal adoration to boot!

And if *one* home in a thousand is saved from the flood, or *one* child in a hundred recovers from some dreadful disease, there is a hallelujah to God-enemy for His mercy so clearly demonstrated—and no one thinks of the thousands who perished. A few hundred crutches have been hung up in a shrine to prove the mercy of Him, but you and I must think of the millions of sick and crippled who succumb daily to the agony of the very same afflictions.

Men still want to appease the God by swaying their beards and praising His grace. Incense and smoke still rise from the altars, and candles are set where they imagine God-enemy to be dwelling, and where with their little offerings (now in coin instead of grain and meat) they hope to appease Him as of old.

Man has learned the use of tools and the art of writing, and from Mother Nature he has learned a bushel of fancy tricks, but his God is still the same gray-bearded stranger riding through the clouds, wielding thunder and lightning and pestilence.

ADONAI ECHOD!

But there is God. Not God-enemy, that sinister Moloch whose sardonic humor blights mankind with calamities and catastrophes, setting deviltry into the hearts of beings and then forever torturing them for acting out His evil design. Such a malevolent God is merely a figment of primitive man's fear-stricken imagination, before which the superstitious have prostrated themselves since time immemorial.

There is God. God, the One majestic idea of our consciousness within this universe, the One without Whom we cannot explain or even comprehend this, our existence, or the life of things—any things; God, without Whom we can neither fathom nor understand the firmament above us in its infinite expanse; God, without Whom we cannot be aware of our cosmic participation in the physical world and our moral participation in the spiritual world; God, of whom the people of ancient Israel wrote: *Adonai Echod!* The Lord is One!

The essence of all Being is One, and there our wisdom ends. But this we feel and know as well as we, with our little souls, can grasp the thought: The way to God is man's love to man.

The sages, from Moses to Spinoza, from Lao-Tse and Buddha to Jesus and Gandhi, brought it out: Man's love to man, and man's love to God are one and the same thing.

It is in our devotion to man that we serve God-Eternal. All other services are incidental or even contrary to the Idea of the One. Man's moral conscience is the gateway to heaven, and his moral deeds the only path to salvation.

If that be not so, then man remains a beast in the jungle of mutual destruction, overwhelming others or succumbing to them, with never the blessings of solace and beatitude—despite occasional prayerful beggings and servile offerings to divinities of the brain that are wishfully harbored there.

THE FLAME

There is an essence in life which is not natural, and yet it is within our nature. Some mystics named it *The Flame;* the Greeks called it *Idea;* the Hebrews, *Ruach;* the Hindus, *Nirvana.*

This consciousness in man's soul of union with the *One* and *All* is the only true religion (binding) to God. There is no God but this One-ness, of whom we know nothing unless we are aware of His reflections in our hearts. If one becomes theological and presumptuous, one runs the danger of straying from the invisible tie between man's soul and man's God.

God has no interpreters but man's hearkening, and the church may or may not speak His voice. The voice of God is too high for some to hear and too low for others, and it does not exist at all for the many, many who are deaf. The voice of God may speak through the morning green of a sun-kissed meadow, the melancholy rhymes of bittersweet poetry, the angry shouts of a dying soldier giving his life on the battlefield altar of freedom, the years of parental drudgery and filial sacrifice, heavenly sermons and songs leaving the lips of the truly inspired, the words of wisdom of sages then and now.

The soul of God is in the soul of man. There is no God but in the consciousness of innermost man.

And *there* is God, the Super-natural, since none of this is "natural" in the sense of the bug-infested jungle rock we call this world of ours. If this our hardbitten, sanguine global existence is nature, then all Divine is beyond nature.

And if these be dreams—our sublime arts and poetic longings, our touch of everlasting wisdom and goodness above the flesh and the self—such dreams must be Divine.

What would be this life of ours were it not for our dreaming in the temples of the Lord?

PROFESSIONALS AT THE ALTAR

When early tribal man killed a lamb or a calf or a child and left it on the altar-stone to appease terrifying God-enemy, even at that period there were some quick-witted bystanders who slyly observed that these sacrifices worked neither way—the feared gods did not devour the proffered flesh and blood, and the fear-stricken people were not blessed with the protection or exemption they sought.

And so the class of professional God-interpreters, priestly usurpers and ghost chasers, was born.

There were often slick ones among the furtive who sensed the muteness of the gods, and these managed to articulate, at first to a few and then to many, the bewildering silences and the stunning contradictions of nature's catastrophes, from the outbursts of volcanoes to floods, from plagues and pestilence to tornadoes and ordinary thunder.

Those sly interpreters understood nature no better than their credulous listeners, except that they sensed these catastrophes had neither rhyme nor reason and occurred in wild disorder. Lightning would never strike twice in the same place, but it would strike the kowtowing just as often as it would the sullen.

So we see in primitive society the rapid rise of two types of men: the self-appointed or hereditary priest or medicine man, and the self-appointed or hereditary chief or strong man.

Since their spheres of maneuver were fundamentally non-competitive, we find them more frequently in mutual supplement than in opposition.

The shaman, pretending prescience and an intimate acquaintance with divine providence, lent heavenly support to the tribal bully or his descendant, without whose strong arm and organization the shaman could hardly have maintained himself for any length of time.

We find this extraordinary set-up throughout ancient history; almost without exception, we meet it in modern history among the primitive tribes of Africa, America and Australia, where medicine man and chief held, and are holding, sway.

It is scarcely surprising to discover that in contemporary Japan the Mikado was pictured by the clergy as a Son of the Sun. We have met this mutual adoration arrangement in ancient Egypt, Babylon, Greece, and so on. A ruthless prince designated as a son of the heavens by a richly endowed clergy is likely to carry on a reign of exploitation for as long as the people's minds are befogged by the cloudy mythology of their altar-keepers.

The theologians of the Christian era are no less culpable than primitive African tribes in this matter of shielding dastardly crowned creatures as "anointed" by the Lord, with whose intentions these theologians have often maintained a caretaker's familiarity.

The theologian knows no more of God than does the peasant, aside from the sly observation that God is mute, while the peasant and the rest of the honest laity feel that the Lord speaks in His deeds and to the bishop.

The bishop of God knows no more than the choir boy, and nearness to the Creator is something entirely different from proximity to the altar. There are no "books of God" but those few that most people have read; all other books are mere arguments among theologians, and if there is a gate to the Lord to be found among the writings of ancient days, the rifts and discussions of the latter-day tractata have all but obliterated it.

The priests and the preachers have no more right to God or knowledge of Him than have the people, and to judge by what the churches of the past have done to the Holy Name, I say the people are to look for Him in their hearts and their consciences, and not in an edifice.

THE BLOODY CHAIN

In nature there may be good and evil, right and wrong, but whose scale is to score the balance? A storm may be wrong for the sailor and just right for the beachcombing islander who is praying for it. A break in a dam is an evil to those trapped in the flats and glens, but it may bring safety to a hard-pressed army.

Nature radiates ever-expanding energies without visible purpose or scope, at least to our judgment and standards. Whole nations perish by war and disaster, the kind and the mean, the hale and the halt, the graybeards and the infants. The generous go to the scaffold and the sinister die in peace. What a tumult and senseless *tohu wa bohu!*

No man of reason can find meaning in the ceaseless, sanguinary battles of all living creatures; there is only the sobering concept that nature operates on a plane completely beyond the reach of man's understanding.

47

By human attitudes and standards, it is horri-
fying to contemplate that living organisms on this
earth are so organized that man lives by devouring bird, and bird by gulping frog, and frog by
swallowing bug, and bug by sucking in lesser insects, and so on. And where there is an animal
eating grain, a pack of carnivorous beasts and
men are waiting to kill it for maw and spit. Beast
eats the animal raw; man, in his refinement, first
singes it, but both are in the very same chain-
hunt of bloody gorging.

There may be good and evil in nature, but by
whose measure? The Good Book says the birds
are being provided for. But what does the worm
say to such Providence? You say your prayers
over the smoldering back of a gentle deer, or the
battered face of a slain enemy soldier. Are the
souls of those two accounted for in the reckoning
of nature's moral equations?

As I write these lines, and as you read them, in
the forests and in the seas, deep in the blackness
of the earthen crust, high in the wind around our
mountains, even in the gills and intestines of men
and beasts, a billion living creatures gnaw and

tear at each other in the predestined gruesome struggle for mere existence. They must kill each other to eat each other, and thus to live! What a devilish scheme of togetherness! What a carnal web of an inescapable bloody chimera!

Such is nature, blind to the light of goodness and deaf to the cry of justice.

If goodness and kindness, fairness and justice, are to come to this world, they must come from man and not from the gods, and if ever man is to hearken to a Lord, He must be nothing but the silent voice that speaks goodness in the heart of man.

There is no God but the One, and He lives in the heart of hearts, whence emanates the breath of spiritual life, the light of humility in this universe, which makes us envision man and world *sub specie aeternitatis.*

From this depth of Godly insight we do not *see* good and evil; we make it. We make the law that divides deeds, intents, and motives in men and nations according to their true value in the glow of our innermost introspection.

We bring light into the blindness of cruel nature, and from the heights of our inspired meditation we bring forth commandments of what man may and may not do. There is no law in nature but that of conquer and devour. But man rises above nature in his attentions and his devotions to that mysterious voice of consciousness of a life far above the common plane, in the realm of compassion and charity, which is as alien to nature as it is close to God.

Adonai Echod! God is One, and the One lives in the heart of man, and the love to God and the love to man are one and the same.

This is not only the beginning of true faith, this is the all of it. The rest is silence.

SHAMANS AND KINGS

The deeds of men may be performed from many motives. For it is in the intent, rather than in the deed itself, that legality or illegality lies.

The watchman who kills a criminal intruder, the robber who cuts down the watchman—they both perform an identical deed, but only one is breaking the law. The motives and purposes determine the law, since actions or omissions in themselves are only incidental.

What, then, are the intents and purposes of the lawmakers, and who are the makers of laws?

One man *by himself* is lawless; law takes effect when man joins man, whether for a short time or permanently. Both men accept the common good as the dominant rule of conduct. However, where there are only two, the will of the stronger will "interpret" the law; where there are many, the will of the most cunning or his successor will prevail. A persuasive or ruthless tribesman may usurp dominance by promises or intimidation, and then fortify and perpetuate his control with the help of an armed clique or a priestly sect. As throne preservers, the shamans of ancient times seem to have been as reliable as the churches of later years, which kept some of the foulest breed of men in hereditary crown and scepter.

As lawmakers are by and large the very same type that grasp for the throne, and since law is determined not by deeds but rather by motives, we must search for the intents of the dominant in order to check on the law.

To cover the obvious, kings and their shamans have frequently resorted to shrouding their deviltry with a cloak of divinity. So successful has been (and is) this camouflage of the singularly unwholesome with the magic of sanctified traditionalism, that merciless acts of wanton torture, slaughter and destruction have been accepted by a thoroughly indoctrinated populace as the blessed measures of an altruistic potentate.

From Pharaoh to Stalin, and from Attila to Hitler, people in mass forgot old reason and reasons, old teachings and teachers, and abandoned themselves to the high spirits of vandalism, convinced that they were doing right by the new law, and that they were doing good by the new faith.

:-:

A law is as proper as the motives of the ruler.

A war is nothing but the mass murder of persons who oppose, or even submit to, the conquering greed of political adventurers. Ethiopians perished because of Mussolini's ambitions, and Koreans died because of Stalin's strategies.

It is these very same usurpers and their shamans who forever reach out for more; their lust becomes patriotism, their greed becomes righteousness, and their ill will becomes law.

Law is as varied as the sentiments of those who rule.

At the time when Americans fought to gain their freedom from the British monarch, the people of England lived under a law that would hang a man or woman for stealing anything valued at ten dollars or more. The law would send a person into bondage to penal colonies for the theft of a loaf of bread. It would sell you as a slave if you were captured as a foreign soldier in war.

At the time of the great Puritan migration, no fewer than two-thirds of the white persons in the New England colonies were living in bondage or some other type of servitude.

Such was the law then.

It was a bitter law, a law that made thieves of the poor, criminals of debtors, and servants of both.

The law is never holy but often sinful. And perhaps even today, in this freest of countries of all times and places, there may be many who stand on the wrong side of the law, placed thus not because they went astray, but rather because the law strayed from the right path.

THE UGLY FENCE

Law originated as a formal expression of one man's servitude to another man, and today in many corners of the world law is still no more than that. The bullying island chief, with or without the help of a group of sanctifying medicine men and sorcerers, can ride roughshod over a kowtowing frenzied tribe, rape their best women and appropriate their best cattle, enlist by promise or threat some of the strong to serve as henchmen—and with the power of shaman and armed guard can lay down the law.

The law is the ugly fence that confines the lowly man in his daily existence, laid down by a conniving or bullying usurper to make the poor, cowed devil do his bidding. This law, enforced by castes of armed henchmen and rationalized by shamans, is a set of prisoners' rules and no more, be it the law of Montezuma, the law of the Maoris, the law of the Pharaohs, the law of Saudi

Arabia, the Marxist code of Russia, the Lex Romana, or the constitution of the Red Republic of China. Be they implied or direct, engraved on clay or written on pulp paper, sworn to by word of mouth or by lips to the cross or the crescent, they are nothing but prisoners' rules of conduct toward the big chief warden, his guards, his chaplains, and, finally, toward each other, for prisoners are property as well as people, and while people are readily expendable by the dominant, those are squeamish about their property.

At close range one finds that throughout history laws may have differed considerably in the details of imperatives and taboos concerning the conduct of prisoners among themselves. But as far as their position with respect to the ruling hierarchy is concerned—be it that of Montezuma or Henry VIII, Stalin or King Saud, Titus or Cleopatra, Hitler or Mao Tse-tung or Louis XIV —it is very much the same: All the power to the bullying or conniving chief, and all the chains to the terrified and shamanized people.

The law was and is just a chain to imprison the masses.

Almost everywhere and at every time, except during brief periods in ancient Israel when a different kind of law, one for the people and not the kings, prevailed; except for the great revolution against the laws of black tradition which began in America and spread through France to Europe, only to be threatened with engulfment by a red-tasseled resurgence of medievalism—almost everywhere and at every time the law has been the ball and chain fettering the serf to his plow and the bonded man to the anvil, the youth to the mercenary's rifle and the sailor to the galley bench, the servant's bride to the lascivious embrace of the lord by the *jus primae noctis* and the fluttering virgin of Arabia to the vanishing sex drives of a foul sheik, the whimpering children of Israel to the gas chambers of a Teutonic dictator and the tortured dissidents of Russia to the Marxist executioner's block.

The law is the sanctification of all the evils of a villainous ochlocracy: it sent a French vagrant to Devil's Island for the theft of a liter of wine; it threw a trembling slave to the lions for the sickly lust of a Messalina; it burned searching, pious souls at the stake; it split the throats of innocent juveniles on the sacrificial altars of priest-begotten Molochs; it massacred millions of deviating comrades, crawling on their knees on the banks of the Yangtze and on the tundras of Siberia.

The law is the crime it purports to prevent.

THE YOKE

There were sometimes men who tried to break the chains of the law. From Moses to Spartacus, from Bar Kochba to Socrates, from Thomas Paine to John Brown, there have been men who rebelled against codes of legalized suppression.

It is the lawbreakers in our history who have brought to the people of the Western world the rights they enjoy, and if the enchained East is to come to its freedom, it will again be the lawbreakers who will tumble the overbearing colossus of lawful totalitarianism.

Rameses and Charlemagne, Genghis Khan and Stalin, Hitler and Mao Tse-tung—they all usurped power and reigned by law, which they either used or created to suit their expansionist drives. Except for the democracies created or influenced by the great American and subsequent French revolutions, the world was and is at the mercy of laws designed by, or inherited from, overbearing political or military chicaneers.

The law-abiding citizen, be he in King Saud's Arabia or Khrushchev's empire, is as bereft of human rights or dignity as the galley slave of Xerxes, the bonded servant of King James I, or the serf of Czar Nicholas.

It is with the crushing of the law that the freedom of man began; the bills of rights were written with the blood of heretics and lawbreakers.

The usurpers have always tried to cloak their laws with sanctimonious gibberish and ribbons of antiquity. This false halo has been ever so effective in awing a naive world, and were it not for the stouthearted few endowed with both vision and altruism, even our own continent might still be under the yoke of their law.

It is one of the peculiarities of man's nature that so very many sane persons actually prefer an existence as subjects of a queen or sheik or party-leader to being masters of themselves and governors of their state by free and effective cooperation.

Such is the magic power of law and its purveyors.

Where will the people go? Along the path of submission to pretentious laws and totalitarian order, or on the road to freedom and self-government?

THE AXE AND THE SCEPTER

War is not in the nature of man; defense is. Ancient, naked man was a grain and root eater, having neither fang nor claw nor swiftness nor the stomach to hunt down, tear apart, and devour other hide-covered animals.

As a herbivorous creature, he had as little instinct to go out and make war against others of his kind as there is in the antelope. When man reached the Tool Age, it is likely that he used sticks and stones to defend himself against other animals. There was still no reason to use weapons against his own kind, for man had nothing to offer man at that stage, and nothing to withhold. Herbs, grains, roots and fruits were probably plentiful and could neither be hoarded nor protected from intruders. When they became scarce, primitive man moved farther afield in search of ants, locusts and other foods within his reach.

When men became tribal, however, possibly

through some natural disaster such as a flood or sudden ice age, and cunning chiefs usurped control of the tribesmen, then war became a means of settling feuds and defending possessions, as well as of obtaining those of other tribes, or their womenfolk, or the tribesmen themselves as slaves.

War is, in this sense, indicative of a higher stage of civilization, where man is no longer a naked grazer and root picker, but a weaponed hunter, herder and grain hoarder. At that stage man no longer lives alone but in a group, and as groups go, the most sly or most strong is likely to exercise a one-man control with the collusion of opportunistic shamans and guards.

War then becomes a means whereby chiefs can increase their power, influence or holdings, and it matters little whether the chief lived a hundred thousand years ago or whether he lived a hundred years ago on a Polynesian island, or whether his name is Napoleon Bonaparte, Mussolini, Stalin, Tamerlane, or Frederick the Great, Peter the Great or Alexander the Great. War is conducted solely for the personal gain, aggrandizement, and conquest-urge of the chief, the people themselves having nothing to gain but an unwanted, measly share of possible loot.

It has always been the policy of war-bent chiefs to incite their own people with the lure of victory and with a gory succession of enemy threats (whether such war excitement is created through war dances accompanied by shamanistic bellowings about lurking enemies, or by refined propaganda transmitted through the latest channels of mass communication).

This preliminary warplay is as important now as it was in the past, and wars are still planned and initiated by one of the tyrants and his entourage of sycophants.

As far as the people themselves are concerned, they have little or nothing to gain by war, but everything—including their lives—to lose. In this sense, war is not in the nature of man, only in the nature of tyranny.

For a hundred thousand years, it is the tyrant who has made wars, although listening to the people's war dances, one might be led to believe they really yearn to be slaughtered or to slaughter others equally misled.

If the conqueror wins, the people share in his loot as a fly shares the meal of a feasting lion; if the conqueror loses, the people carry the burden of guilt and responsibility.

So it was in the ancient days, and in the days of Hitler and Stalin. The conquerors gloried in martial splendor when they were advancing, but the common people were left to pay reparation when they were on the run.

THE MANY, THE FEW
AND THE ONE

If one were to stand on a hill a thousand miles afar and focus his eyes upon our cities, he doubtless would conclude that man is but of one kind—black, brown or yellow, but one.

Yet mankind divides itself into three distinct types:

The *Opportunists* who fail to comprehend our dreamlike and so brief life-awareness on this whirling, mossy rock. They imagine this span as real, using all the paraphernalia of faith and heritage to exploit the naive and groping. They are the usurpers and pushers, the confidence men of politics and religion, business and even art. They are the godless amongst the fearful and faithful, the unprincipled who make success their principle. They are the Nizams and the Commissars, the Caesars and Sheiks, the Metternichs and the Richelieus. They live their fill of life by making hasty conquests of their fellow dwarfs, collecting metals and little rocks raised to high value by silent agreement of the various international cliques. Like a flash, the few decades given to man vanish, and the sorcerers of opportunism bite the dust. How much evil, though, can be done in so little time! A thousand volumes could be filled reciting man's inhumanities to man at the behest of greedy opportunists. They have marched over corpses, through forests of gallows, toward the flush of power, just to sink into the grave from a throne instead of a chair. *Vanitas, vanitatum, vanitas.* And this vanity of command and gold has been and still is degrading the world of man to a life of competitive bloodshed ever since time was counted.

This granite earth we live on could be a bed of roses were it not for the scheming Procrustes and his fellows.

There always have been amongst the many a few who are conscious of the mysterious All about us, the rhythm of the universes in which we are but a tiny pebble, and our existence of fleeting dream in eternity.

This second type of being is the *Man of Conscience*. He does not join in the chase for opportunities, but seeks for himself and others a place of serenity. And as he desires no more for himself than he does for others, he seeks community and cooperation, instead of conquest and competition. And as he is constantly aware of man's closeness to the end from the very beginning, he cries out to those who are unaware to hearken to the voice of the heavens and behold the majesty of the universe. The Hebrews called such men "Announcers," "Teachers," (Prophets).

These men have always been among us. The voice of God speaks through the lips of these men and in the conscience of our own hearts. The conscience in us is more than the voice of God; it is God Himself, since without our conscience there would be a billion rocks storming aimlessly through space and time, and we riding on one of them, a mere mold on its surface.

Man's conscience is his bridge to eternity. What else is there to tie us to our ancestors, to our descendants, and to fellow man? In serving fellow man, we serve the only true God we know, the One and the Eternal, the Nameless One Whose Nature is Love.

The nature of God is love, and the nature of man is in devotion to it.

So we have three types of man: The Opportunist, the Man of Conscience, and *The Many.* I say *The Many;* what name can you give those who sit at the feet of the prophet one day, and parrot the greedy shrieks of the usurpers tomorrow?

The Many are those not distinguished by either drive or meditation. Their weakness is the tyrant's strength, and their strength is the prophet's consolation.

Generations come and go and with them change the masters of opportunity, driving man against man and nation against nation in their blasphemous lust for power. Their slogans change as do their war dances, but it is the same devil behind the mask of gold.

The voice of the prophet is still announcing the coming of a better life, established on the peace and strength of man's conscience. Will ever the quietude of the Messiah win over the turmoil of opportunistic clamor?

:-:

Will silence win over the shriek? Will God banish Lucifer forever?

The issue is still in doubt, but hope will live on with charity and love.

The Greater Self

Man's axe got sharper, not his wit.

:-:

If you have not made your mark on this world, you have never lived.

:-:

The hermit is a dull man preoccupied with nothing but his little self—be it physical, be it spiritual. The wise man, like Socrates, seeks out the people of the world and makes them part of his own self, the greater Self of the greater man.

:-:

To love people is to know them.

:-:

Human conscience is the only true moral guide, since all so-called ethical precepts, as well

as religious commands, may be—and have been
—turned as easily to evil as to good.

:-:

Knowledge *may* be good; kindness *is* good.

:-:

Leave this world the way you found it: a
heap of suffering and a drop of blessing. Don't
run out without the latter—so many do.

:-:

If not for the conscience in some of the people,
I would despair of all of them.

:-:

Man is more often chained by a web of slavish
ideas than by metal links.

:-:

The recluses, those who run into the desert or
into the forest to fight their sins, never do they
conquer. They are only hiding from the enemy.
To win, one must face the enemy in the light of
the day and in the turmoil of open battle.

72

Byways of Reason

Misnamed faculty of the mind: ability to focus attention on a task in the future, commonly referred to as *memory*, a proper term for remembering images of the past. A person may have excellent retention of past images and still lack the admirable talent for bringing to his mind a certain subject at a given time on the morrow. Such a one can remember perfectly detailed events gone by, and not "remember" to meet an obligation in the nearest future. The latter attribute of calling to one's mind duties which one has undertaken to perform, is a faculty entirely distinct from *re-membering*, although constantly referred to as such.

:-:

The professional man, oftener than not, fails to see the forest for the trees; hence, so many basic discoveries in medicine and other sciences were made by outsiders and laymen.

:-:

It is the seemingly obvious that is most puz-

73

zling to the philosopher, and, by the same token, the most puzzling seems obvious to the common man.

:-:

Thought is a twig on the tree of emotion and instinct. As it was a million years ago, the first is still an outgrowth of the latter.

:-:

The first great step lies in recognizing the importance of reason; the second, so much more difficult, is to recognize reason's limitations.

:-:

Knowledge is found within the subject and not outside. A tiny leaf of grass hides a thousand secrets: the riddle of its growing, of its taking on color, of its absorbing rays of the sun, and other bodies, of its feeding on gases and minerals, and so on, *ad infinitum*. It is, as all is, microcosmos, a splinter of the universe with all the mysteries of its own substance.

:-:

The semblance of reason is often more attractive than reason itself.

The world still has not learned that although a man may be a great mathematician, his ideas on politics or poetry carry no more weight than those of a cobbler.

:-:

It takes a lot of knowledge to understand how little we know.

:-:

Thinking is a luxury of the mind; most people stick to the necessities.

:-:

If all the people who have the capacity to think would do so, this civilization would be a thousand years further along.

:-:

Did you ever take time out to think? People take time out to lunch, to swim, to loaf, to fish, to dance, to play, to pray, to paint, even to make love. But did you ever take time out to think? And I do not mean to think about your business or your personal affairs, but to think about the nature of things and the nature of man.

Knowledge makes man neither free nor good. The Romans, most learned of ancient peoples, tolerated Caligula and Nero, and enthusiastically carried the scourge of the Fasces into peaceful neighboring lands. The Germans, most learned of the twentieth century, elected a paranoic housepainter as chancellor and tumbled gleefully from executions to death-camps and back.

Knowledge and science are tools that can be used for evil as readily as for the good. The scientist or scholar is not made a better man by his knowledge, only a more dangerous one.

:-:

Goodness stems not from knowing, but from *willingness of the heart.* It is the voice of the conscience that makes man free and kind, and nothing else. In many, this voice has been stilled by selfish and brutal upbringing.

Education in physics, mathematics, egocentric history tests, etc., will sharpen the wit, not soften the heart. We are in dire need, not of teachers of the brain, but of teachers of the heart.

Education in conscientious living will change the face of mankind; knowledge alone will only reshape the grimace.

:-:

Controversy frequently divulges little about the issues at stake, but much about the motives of those disagreeing.

:-:

Logic is the intricate pattern of our thought processes, awareness of which we have only in words and symbols. What sail as books on logic or theory of knowledge are for the most part dissertations on grammar, syntax and semantics, or words, words, words. From Aristotle to Husserl, the logical systems have been systems of words rather than of facts. The mechanism of man's soul escapes those who search for truth among the verbal traces of the mind.

:-:

Reason is the aptitude to examine a proposition as to correctness of premise without being influenced by established prejudices or traditional thought patterns.

The thought-processes of most people run un-reasonably along deepset ruts of hearsay, pensay, churchsay, clubsay, schoolsay, guttersay, parlor-say and smart wishsay.

Among those thickly planted weeds there is pitifully little room for reason to flourish.

If they would only stop to think—nay, rethink every little premise they have been carrying in the mental toolchest as a true measure of facts. Man's conclusions are so desperately inadequate because his sprawling network of premises is all twisted.

You cannot pass just judgment if your book of rules is nothing but a muddled set of selfishly nurtured prejudices and wishful misbeliefs.

:-:

There is no knowledge—only a lesser state of ignorance.

:-:

Logic is ever so often the handmaiden of prejudice.

:-:

Only the vain feel misunderstood; the wise expect it.

The truly wise are always simple. It is the little mind that spins complications.

Only About God

The pagans had a god for the winds, the waves, and the flames, but the Jews had a god for the *conscience*. The pagan god was fear-born; Jehovah was born a light of the inner soul.

:-:

Man lived a million years without God, and when he found Him his worship changed, but his beastliness hardly.

:-:

The limitations of human understanding are the beginnings of faith.

:-:

People need religion because they are lazy of spirit. You have to bring them God on the altar;

79

they would not walk to him directly. Does God deserve such people?

:-:

You have laughed God out of your schools, out of your books, and out of your life, but you can not laugh Him out of your death.

You still do your three score and ten, and then sink into dust knowing not the why and wherefore of this fleeting dream-trot in the arena of the human anthill.

:-:

If nature had a plan to protect its creatures from being exterminated, why did it give them an appetite for each other? Again, if nature made the grasshopper green to have it melt into the green of the grass, why did it paint the horse on the same ground a shiny brown or black or striped, like the zebra? And why the seal, black on the snowy backdrop, and the parrot red and yellow?

To our sense and reason, all this makes no logic; by what calculation it does, I do not know.

Man imagining that the universe evolved as a pedestal for his perfection is like a breath taking the storming winds as God-sent carriers of his vapor.

:-:

The further one travels on the ocean of knowledge, the greater looms the horizon of the Unknown.

:-:

Maybe you can worship God in a thousand ways, but never with racks and faggots. Maybe you can serve socialism in a thousand ways, but never with axeman's block and death-camps.

:-:

There are a thousand problems urging the searching soul to faith in much more knowledge than little everyday scientific intelligence can supply.

Faith is nothing but knowledge that what we understand is only a shadow of the Unknown. Faith is the science of the pitiful limitations of man's mental scope.

In this sense, the wise and knowing like Socrates, Newton, Spinoza and Einstein were the great Faithful.

Conscience is God's imprint on the soul of man. Those who live merely by shrewd opportunism and have no ear for the conscience within have been bypassed by the gods, be they men in high posts or men posted low.

:-:

The Jews are a little but stubborn ancient tribe whom the Western world can not forgive because they gave it their God, Jehovah, and His Bible, His only Son, the Prophets and the Apostles, sweet mother Mary and the four Jews who wrote the New Testament of Christ and His Church.

If the Jews had done nothing more they should have been revered in all places of Christian worship instead of being maligned. If it was willed by Providence for some Jews to ask for the trial of Christ, it was at the same time given to other Jews to be His Faithful and Apostles.

The Church of Christ was a church in Israel and of Israelites long before it became a church of the world.

The Gregarious Creature

There is a bit of slave instinct still in almost every man—perhaps, like the evolutionary gills, a carry-over from the primitive ages when all were slaves except the pharaoh and his priest.

This bit of slave instinct is what the communist schemers count on in their propagation of absolute submission to the Party bosses and Party ukases. This relic of a slave era is the only possible explanation for the undeniable success of a ruthless oligarchy, even among intellectuals who must know that all they have to gain from communism is a chance to be shackled.

:-:

Fanciful ideologies have often served ambitious imperialists and their epigones as camouflage, and even motivation, of their will to conquer.

:-:

Torquemada made the same use of all-loving Christ as Hitler did of purity-loving National

Socialism, or Stalin did of humanity-loving communism. Those three, as well as the others of their intent, cut down mercilessly millions of the innocent while preaching their ideological love-schemes. O Love, thy color is *red!*

:-:

The basic difference between man and dog leaving a forest lies in the dog's devouring the local animals skin and all, while man sets the bones aside. It is by the bones that you can tell the difference, as any woodsman will vouch and little else.

:-:

Some persons make such great efforts preparing themselves for life, as if they were to go on living for a thousand years. They are so busy getting ready that they hardly get to living.

Adverse and Universe

Some of the most fascinating writers on geographica never left their studies, like Kant, Jules Verne, May. Others have travelled all over the globe—and seen nothing.

:-:

Sentiment is the dew that drops from the clouds of melancholy.

:-:

Reality—what a poor substitute for imagination!

:-:

Friendship is a prize you have to earn. The incorrigibly hopeful expect it to fall into their laps; it never does.

:-:

Why does the Bible tell man that the animal is his meat? Did ancient man hesitate to stray from grain and fruit?

:-:

Man sometimes lives, but constantly dies. *Semper morituri sumus.*

The greatest gift is the art of giving.

:-:

If you failed to learn ethics at six, you will not learn it at sixty.

:-:

Wish they would prune people, as they do trees, of their dead and overgrown twigs.

:-:

A giraffe may speak louder than a mule, were our ears in tune with his voice.

:-:

Love is never wasted; it will come back to you some day.

:-:

Love and hate are of the same coin, just two sides of it.

:-:

The greatest number of books have been written about whom we know the least: Jesus Christ.

:-:

If a man writes for posterity, look not for him in the list of fashionable bestsellers.

Little uglinesses fill the air of our society like insects. They don't kill you, but they make life miserable.

:-:

We are all laymen, only some more so than others.

:-:

Fear is the severest of pains, and the least alleviated.

:-:

Things are things—the riddles lie in man.

:-:

Philosophy is the awareness of man's minuteness in the great infinite.

:-:

Real friendship you can only make when you are very young, and then again when you are very old.

:-:

Poets are daydreamers of the soul. Who says that a dreamer must look the part? He may be a clerk, and dream like a prince; she may be a schoolmarm, and wonder like a Pompadour.

:-:

Children may be little, but they are people.

:-:

The little sins catch even the saints unprepared.

:-:

Perhaps our fear of death is but embryonic fear of life.

:-:

An alibi is easily found by the lethargic or indolent.

:-:

Being forever sweet may be as much a false front as being forever gruff.

:-:

Don't look for depth in a shallow mound.

:-:

A play full of action—and nothing else.

Sometimes our adversaries cut our road, compelling us to take another—and frequently, better —direction. Thus, we owe a certain bizarre gratitude to our enemies.

:-:

Reminiscing in free thought-association (as practiced by analysts) about infantile experiences and upset-stomach dreams will as little cure a sick mind as it will heal an ailing liver or broken leg.

:-:

Faith has its weaknesses, but faithlessness is the poorest substitute.

:-:

A fool lacks both a sense of humor and a sense of puzzlement.

:-:

In reading, sometimes less is more.

:-:

Sarcasm is the defense of the ill-talented.

:-:

The late-sleeping cocks crow the loudest.

Hasty thinking made no philosopher.

:-:

A fast plow rides the surface.

:-:

The thought of Life seldom occurs but at the time of death.

:-:

Sentiment has become an opprobrium in an age which confuses indolence with fortitude.

:-:

Homesickness for childhood toys or village is but the yearning of disillusioned age for the dream world it once held possible.

:-:

It is still sweet to die for your fatherland if it houses freedom.

:-:

Music: the echo of the songs of the gods. All music is either worship or just noises, be they pleasant or dissonant.

:-:

Advice is frequently no more than an expression of the person giving it; he can see no further point than the one he is trying to make.

:-:

Time moves in an uneven tempo, slow to the childlike and primitive mind, rapid to the adult and cogitating. To a child, one day is a long, long time; to the grown-up, a day is quickly gone.

:-:

Leisure is given by society to those who hate their work, who set up intricate methods of killing their "spare" time by hobbies, sports and sundry other devices.

:-:

We see nothing clearer in others than our own weaknesses.

:-:

They pay more attention to bugs on vegetables than bugs infesting man.

:-:

What we need is not a new Messiah but better acquaintance with the old ones.

Nothing ties people closer than common prejudices.

:-:

We make heroes to suit our childish daydreams.

:-:

A potato vine without beetle and rot will still grow a potato. Man, after all diseases are conquered (and in time they will be), still remains only a frail creature of three-score and ten.

:-:

If you come down to earth, how primitive this all is, life between boulders overgrown with plants, and that immense white-hot rock, euphemistically poeticized as "the Sun," life in an ocean of oxygen, nitrogen and other gases, without which neither plant nor animal could endure, and in which we seem to exist in order to gnaw at each other's vitals.

:-:

Life is what you *see* in it. Without your eyes and mine, the swaying tree is but another speck in the fathomless universe, your most beloved just another breath, and all your science and order a mere game in the fleeting life-span of germ- and worm-beset puny creatures to whom their split seconds of conscious pushing about seem like substantial reality in time and space.

:-:

As we found the way to transform elements, we may some day decipher the manner in which matter comes to life, and then perhaps discover that our greatest mystery is only one tiny secret in the immense universe.

:-:

Even the lowly animals have senses we lack: The cow will find a spring or waterhole within a ten-mile radius; man could perish from thirst a hundred feet away from an unseen spring. A pigeon will find its way fifty miles from home; man will run in circles, in shouting distance from his goal. A bat flies by sound signals which we can not hear.

These are just some of the commonplace

senses strange to us; there are scores of others among curious creatures, less familiar but no less baffling, and many more of which we are not even aware. The wisdom of the body is manifold, manifest in the million plants as well as animals, sucking their respective variations of oxygen, hydrogen, nitrogen and other gases—a thousand talents in this gas-enlivened world.

A roach lived in a clock and thought it knew all the secrets of the world because it watched and listened until it could foretell each tick.

:-:

Perhaps our own world with its noble planets and stars is just a bit of empty space in the grand scheme of the unfathomed universe. So tiny are the whirling galaxies compared to the billions of miles of in-between space, that these coordinated globes of ours are little better than specks of dust in an almost vacancy.

How far can we see? Only ether and rock! Look into the flaming gases of the sun and wonder what is beyond that fiery ocean, what is yonder, far in the limitless extension of our own frail concepts of space? What worlds are rising in the far sky? Here with us are mere gases and stony spheres; what fills the unknown distances of the Past-horizon we may not even guess. We are bereft of means of cogitation on celestial eternities; to our frame of mind, the suns and their fields must set as well as travel in bordered realms.

But where are the borders of the nebulae, and what looms or sinks *outside?* How circumscribed a vision ours is! Neither can we conceive of a borderless extension of the galaxies, nor can we fit the All inside a fence.

Still, we may dream, dream of the worlds that lie beyond the flaming sun and beyond the billions of stars.

:-:

Perhaps, where the darkness of our envisioned space comes to an end, perhaps in that Past-horizon, new worlds are living in fantastic panoramas—valleys stretched out far and deep in new colors of magnificent beauty, higher creatures of rare character, so different from our common lot that walk like men and live like beasts.

That realm of the Past-horizon may have the blessing of knowing God and themselves whole; we live only in fear of God, strangers to ourselves.

:-:

Even if we were to unravel all the puzzles of our visible world, answer all the gaping queries of matter and energy, we still would be not much better off than the virus injected into the egg yolk, acting up in clever reflexes after having travelled through the multiple layers of plasm, which must have seemed to the virus a million miles in as many years.

We may never manage even to touch cosmic knowledge, the understanding of what is in the Past-horizon, but at least we may feel the baleful grip of our earthbound limitations.

:-:

It is not earth that is mother of man, but the sun. The sun gives its nourishing rays to the

plants which man and his animal-food live on;
the sun evaporates the water that filters into
man's springs; the sun warms the air man
breathes and the ground he walks on. Man is
truly a child of the sun. Still, whence does Helion
draw its matter and energy? Wherefrom the unknown and perhaps peregrine donor?

:-:

The common man may be confronted with the
same questions as a thinking man—the difference
lies in the dissatisfaction of the latter with a quick
or handy reply. Ancient average opinion held
that the heavens hung by divine fetters; mod-
erns speak of gravities holding each planet like
Münchausen pulling himself up from the mud by
his own boots.

It takes a lot of thought to fathom human
knowledge, and rare intellectual humility to real-
ize that the greatest depth of man's thinking still
runs only in shallow grooves of this mysterious
cosmos.

:-:

Man is as much the crown of creation as a

gourd of water. It is sheer self-deception to pretend that this water-inflated, bug-infested, carnivorous, murderous, greedy human is better than other animals that are born much as he is, and die much as he does, but create less terror and less bloodshed.

:-:

Perhaps the tick on the head of a lamb cogitates that the rain falls so the grass can grow to feed the sheep it pesters. Our prayerful processions for rain are not too far from the tick mentality.

:-:

The evolutionist is plagued by the troubles of the Bible scholar: Where did Cain get his wife if he was the only man's son? And where did the first "thing" come from, whence all the rest of the world evolved?

:-:

We are nutritional satellites of the sun. It feeds the plants that feed the animals that feed us. As for the moon, perhaps its other side, which we have never seen, carries a secret.

With all his complications, man still lives for the three primate goals: food, shelter, and sex. And for such goals, he kills more now than in the Stone Age.

:-:

Without our dreams, this is just an anthill, where only the six-legged ones live in harmony.

:-:

Wars are ordered by the lords, and paid for by the serfs.

:-:

Wars of independence are but the inverted will for peace.

Giant Shadows and Small Men

Any fool can see the fallacies of previous generations; to recognize those of his own takes great power of discernment.

:-:

We are bound in time and space like a spool at

the spinner's; we move up and down, and right and left, as the pattern dictates. Perhaps the spool also thinks it is travelling under its own power in its chosen direction.

:-:

Some of those buried in prison yards deserved mausoleums, and many of those entombed in cathedral sepulchres should have been thrown to the jackals. The tombstone tells when you died, not how you lived.

:-:

Death is but birth in reverse: the extinction of bio-energy, which carries the shape of a man, the instinct of a million years, and finally the cruel limitations of life-span, from an invisible seed to wilting senectitude.

:-:

We are still living in a society where most persons have no opportunity to develop their minds to the fullest extent. The great machine of the world-mind is running on just a few of its cylinders.

Beware of the reformer who uses his platform merely as a pedestal for his own little ego. The world has always had those who take on the voice of God, and sound off for themselves—those with the cunning tongues who, in depicting the Lord's celestial abode, never fail to point out their own right of eminent domain there.

:-:

So many of the great patriots were and are men of age. Men whose life is flowing away caress the beloved nation of which they are a part. It is in the love of his people that mortal man never dies.

:-:

Faculties of the sciences change in public importance with the times. At present, physics is at the peak because of its military importance; a generation ago, social science rode the crest of popularity, and prior to that, engineering. There was a long and much-maligned period when theology was the queen of the sciences, and I doubt if our epoch of nucleonics enthroned is a step to a higher existence. Perhaps tomorrow the bac-

teriologist will ascend the throne of world signifi-
cance on a novel scheme of germ or virus war
plans.

:-:

Our sages said that when the Torah was written even the Lord kept silent. When some of our
books are written, it seems as if a score of little
devils were at work, chattering blood, lust, crime,
torture, and circumspect perversion. These are
not books, but mere throw-aways for lowdown
amusement. One is uncertain whether vulgar au-
thors wish to please a common public, or a fal-
tering audience is stepping down to the pitiful
level of pen hacks.

:-:

Literacy is a dubious indication of civilization.
The Imperial Romans, loaded with literacy, lived
on the sweat and blood of the world, a bestial
scourge of humanity whose ultimate pleasures
were carnal abominations in their foul arenas.
However, at the same time, in the gentle lands of
the Incas, a refined system of social brotherhood
prevailed among people, none of whom could
read or write.

The European discovered Asia with its spices, woods, and pearls, but he left Asia's greatest treasure almost untouched—her literature and philosophy. It is only now that Western man realizes he looked in the wrong chest.

:-:

No creed is so firm that it permits not interpretation for sinister purposes. Even the sweet tongue of Jesus was made to speak for the devil of bigotry, intolerance, and suppression.

:-:

The red-shirted flag-bearer of the hammer and sickle is brother under the skin to the brown-shirted flag-bearer of the swastika.

:-:

The Red camarilla has taken the romance out of socialism and replaced it with opportunistic expedience, thus losing the best of the idea and acquiring the worst that is in imperialist government.

:-:

Peace with the devil remains always a one-sided arrangement.

Hunting, and fishing as well, are a sheepish return to the primitive instinct to kill. Wormy deer are shot for the prize of horns, bear for a decorative skin, and fish for the sake of a tale. "Good sport" to decadent people, but the old blood-dripping jaw to harmless grazers.

:-:

Art is the talent of giving meaning to nature's creations, be they human, animal, plant or horizons. Non-objective art uncovers the flight of broken little souls from the grandeur and majesty of the heavens to the nothingness of dots and lines.

:-:

Around the core of real art floats a motley crowd of pretentiously bearded painters with their sandalized female entourage, hollow-cheeked unpublished versifiers, and writers completing a never-ending novel.

Of late, there have been so many of these pretenders invading our parlors and our resorts that the real artists are almost embarrassed to admit to their profession.

It seems the Greeks wrote history with little respect for the bearded Asiatics, to whom they rather contemptuously referred as barbarians. The Romans, on the other hand, were so impressed by the Greeks that they hardly ever questioned their authenticity, and the Western world has until this day pretty much accepted the Greco-Roman interpretation of materia philosophica, allowing, of course, an unimpeded path to Judeo-Christian theology.